Edith
the
Good

ALL IN THE FAMILY

Contributing Writers

NORMAN LEAR
DON NICHOLL
MICHAEL ROSS
BERNIE WEST
MILT JOSEFSBERG
LOU DERMAN
BILL DAVENPORT
LARRY RHINE
MEL TOLKIN
HAL KANTER

HARVE BROSTEN
RON FRIEDMAN
BARRY HARMAN
SUSAN PERKIS HAVEN
DON KLEIN
MICHAEL LEESON
SAM LOCKE
GORDON MITCHELL
WARREN S. MURRAY
STANLEY RALPH ROSS
LLOYD TURNER
OLGA VALLANCE
STEVE ZACHARIAS

Edith the Good

The Transformation of Edith Bunker
from Total Woman to Whole Person

SPENCER MARSH

HARPER & ROW PUBLISHERS

New York Hagerstown

San Francisco London

*Dedicated
to all those who are helping me to see
but especially to
Doris
who when I can't see
suffers me still and guides
me in my blindness.*

FIRST EDITION

Designed by C. Linda Dingler

Library of Congress Cataloging in Publication Data

Marsh, Spencer.
  Edith the Good.
  1. All in the family. 2. Women—Psychology.
3. Self-actualization (Psychology) I. Title.
PN1992.77.A483M3   791.45'7   76–62943
ISBN 0–06–065420–1
ISBN 0–06–065421–X pbk.

Contents

Foreword

A television network official defined "All in the Family" as more than just a success, a hit, or a smash. He called it an explosion. That meant it evoked such fierce loyalty that people would plan their social lives around it. I know because countless fans would say to me, "We never go out Saturday nights any more." Or, "We don't leave the house Saturday nights until we've seen 'All in the Family.'"

In my career I never before had been part of an explosion. I had been a featured supporting player in successful Broadway shows, and in many audience-pleasing plays on tour and in summer theatres. These brought enough recognition to lead me to rather obscure roles in New York-based television. Then along came Norman Lear and his original pilot script of "All in the Family." My reaction when I first read it was amazed delight . . . "but this on television?!" It took three tryout readings before the part was mine. Norman gave me an important clue to help me audition. He said that Edith could shut out Archie's abuse. Through years of Archie's uninhibited tirades of egocentric bigotry, Edith had learned to turn him off. This was an actable clue and gave me what I needed to win the role. From such seeds do full-blown characters grow.

Meanwhile, the explosion was reverberating in my life, pushing me into instant fame. Carlyle says, "Fame is no sure test of merit, but only a probability of such; it is an accident, not a property of men." I love that!

So much for my fame. But I am not so sure Edith Bunker's fame is as coincidental. She has endeared herself to millions and may never be forgotten. Her durability lies in her ineffable spirit which has so touched millions that as her interpreter I receive the love she evokes. Often I am approached with the words, "We just *love* you." I bathe in the warmth but know it is Edith they love.

It's natural for me to speak of Edith Bunker objectively, since there are two identities there on the television screen: Edith Bunker and Jean Stapleton. They are distinct. They can never merge even though they seem to. It always surprises me when fans expect me to walk like Edith, talk like Edith, and even run like Edith.

In the beginning Edith evolved in my own imagination, in that of the producers-writers, the director, and ultimately that of the viewers. The show is seven years old now, and Edith lives in the imagination of a different creative staff. The familiarity of a favorite TV show causes the viewer to forget that each character is being portrayed by an actor. The actor is like an artist. He or she paints, delineates, brings to full dimension the character set down by the writer. The maturing of the character is a collaboration among the writers, actors and director. The writer expects the actor to flesh out what he has set down. For example, Edith's run evolved in rehearsal. Having lived in New York City most of my life, I know that people often live under the pressure of time. So I placed Edith under that pressure. Archie compounds it with his demands for her service: "Bring me a beer!" "Dinner on the table at six o'clock!" Hence her dutiful run.

I am proud that Spencer Marsh has found Edith Bunker a useful springboard for his tribute and counsel to women. I am also glad that it is a man who has articulated a vision of the whole woman. As he simply and eloquently promotes woman's right to wholeness in this book, he suggests that equality between the sexes will be a fact when man discovers more of his "womanhood" and woman her "manhood."

To me feminism is not a battle of the sexes. Rather it is an emerging consciousness in the people God has made—a more divine view of unity replacing a limiting, mortal view of separateness from God and from each other. "Male *and* female created He them" (Gen. 1:27). The whole person is one of either gender who possesses masculine *and* feminine qualities, not masculine *or* feminine.

This sexual revolution of thought has displaced many myths in my mind. Consider the one that assigns intuition only to women. Have you ever met a man endowed with this quality? I have—many. Or the myth that says only a man can be dispassionate and objective about a problem. Not so! I know women who deal with problems everyday in this way. Have you seen men giving loving care to their children as tenderly as any mother? Or women disciplining and guiding their children with the intelligence of fatherhood?

It's an adventure to discover the myths, separate them from the truth, and shatter them. What do men and women need most to accomplish this? Native wisdom and love, which as Edith has demonstrated, is independent of intellect, culture, or education. Edith is a fiction—none of us is Edith—but the humanity she represents is real. With that, we can lift our vision to a more complete sense of man *and* woman.

JEAN STAPLETON

Los Angeles, Calif.

Preface

These last months I expected anyone that I told I was writing this book to ask why I, a man, was doing a book about women. Even though I am sure some wanted to, nobody asked. I wish they had because I have some important and personal reasons I would like to share.

First, I am a *former* male chauvinist, trying to live out a style of equality with women which I believe to be right. This book is part of the process that has made me think through many of the implications.

Then, I live with and love four women: Doris, my wife, and our three teen-age daughters, Wendy, Sharee, and Julie. I wish for them the highest quality of life, including equal opportunity with men. In some areas of our society they will be penalized for being female. I don't like that, and I want it to change.

As a pastor-counselor, I have seen many women who are victimized by their families and society in the same way that Edith Bunker often is. I hope this book will help and encourage all who find themselves in Edith's predicament—living with a stifler or stifler*s*.

Finally, I just wanted to write a book about Edith Bunker. I love her. In this I am not alone as I have discovered while doing radio and TV shows across our country talking about my earlier book *God, Man, and Archie Bunker.* Many shared with me what fans you are also.

I have a special advantage though, for I have the privilege of knowing the actress who created Edith, Jean Stapleton, a beautiful human being. I am thankful to her for time and support as I am to Norman Lear, the show's producer, and Virginia Carter, vice-president of public affairs, and all the creative writers who produce some of TV's best scripts.

Thanks also to my good friend and typist, Ruth Arterberry, and, last but not least, to Doris Burke Marsh, my wife and researcher. We made a contract that she do the research for the book which was a new kind of relationship for us. She was really more than a researcher though because we discussed many ideas in the book during the writing. Some discussions became personal struggles but worth it. I thank her for hanging in there and helping me see the woman's side when I was blind.

And you, dear reader, thank you for picking up the book and listening.

SPENCER MARSH

Edith
the
Good

"At the dim extreme of the light of Liberty."

1

Grace under Pressure

There is a land that has in its harbor gateway the statue of a woman who symbolizes liberty. In that same land there is another woman for whom liberty, in any personal way, is but a dream. This woman lives at the dim extreme of the light cast by the Statue of Liberty's hand-held torch. Rather than being guided by the light of liberty, she is disabled by two words bellowed by her husband and pressed upon her by much of society: Stifle yourself! The woman is Edith Bunker, wife and mother of television's "All in the Family." She represents many real women who live in all our neighborhoods.

Edith Bunker, in spite of her stifling environment, does not come on as the complete victim but rather, as one of her fans says, "grace under pressure." Inherent kindness and deep personal integrity undergird the beautiful simplicity of her personality.

That simplicity shows itself in everything from her little keepsake jewel box with its Cracker Jack ring and high-school prom corsage to the easy explanations she has for those who question her.

Edith. I don't really believe in astrology, but it's fun to know what's going to happen, even if it don't.

Edith. I'm not superstitious, Archie, You can't say that I believe in chain letters. I just don't believe in taking chances.

Unlike many of her peers, Edith is open to change even though the things that accompany change are hard for her. When there was a meat shortage and her daughter, Gloria, prepared horse meat for supper, Edith became ill.

Gloria. Ma, why're you so upset?
Edith. I keep thinking of Mr. Ed.
Gloria. Ma, we're not eating Mr. Ed. Ma, people have been eating horse meat in the rest of the world for years.
Edith. Yeah . . . but Gloria—a horse!! People ride on horses. The queen rides on a horse.
Gloria. Ma, it's no different from eating a chicken.
Edith. But the queen don't ride on a chicken.

Keeping up with the times for Edith includes keeping up with the woman's movement, and when she can't, her reasoning is still in the context of simplicity:

Mike. Did you go to your woman's meeting?
Edith. Oh, no. With all the shoppin', washin' and housecleaning I didn't have time to be liberated today.

To speak of the beautiful simplicity of Edith's personality is not to suggest that life is easy for her. Edith lives in a stifling environment personified by the man with whom she lives, loves, eats, and sleeps—her husband, Archie Bunker. Not realizing Scripture gives other options, he is the fulfillment of Genesis 3:16: "Her desire shall be for her husband and he shall lord it over her." Archie seems to remember only one word from their wedding vows—*obey*—and obedience seems to be about all he expects from Edith.

She is supposed to stifle when he says stifle and move when he says move. Meals are to be prepared and on the table at times he establishes, and when he calls for his beer, she is to have it there. She does all this at the roadrunner's pace. One has to agree with Father Majiski. When he found out his new friend was married

"I didn't have time to be liberated today."

to Archie Bunker, he said, "You know, Mrs. Bunker, all things considered you're a remarkably cheerful woman."

So she is, but as a counselor who has talked with many women who in one way or another identify with Edith, I am convinced that she also suffers great periods of anguish. She has suffered them for a number of years, and now they are in danger of increasing. The findings of Dr. Pauline Bart explain this concern:

The traditional woman bases her self-esteem on a role, motherhood, that she must finally relinquish. Some do this with ease; some others . . . cannot. But the problem is not hers alone; society has provided no guidelines for her, no rites of passage. The empty nest, then, may prompt the extreme feelings of worthlessness and uselessness that characterize depressives. One can think of these women as overcommitted to the

maternal role and then, in middle age, suffering the unintended conse-
quences of this commitment.

... my data shows that it is the women who assume the *traditional*
feminine role—who are housewives, who stay married to their husbands,
who are not overtly aggressive, in short, who accept the traditional norms
—who respond with depression when their children leave.[1]

Much of that last paragraph describes Edith. Daughter Gloria
married but still lived at home, and that helped ease the pain.
Gloria's first move was just next door, and so the real trauma of
separation was again avoided. Nevertheless, some day she will,
in all probability, move away, and Edith will hurt. If she tries to
ease the pain by stepping out of her home into the world, she will
discover that her labor is worthless, her ability is considered
limited, and her rights are less than those enjoyed by half the
population, all because she is a woman. She will continue to hear
the words she has heard much of her life: Stifle yourself.

What do you say to a stifled, hurting human being? Very little.
You certainly don't preach at them. Yet there is a liberating,
freeing word to be shared with any stifled woman. That word is
permission, a term used by transactional analysts. It means allowing yourself to be freed of the broken records that keep going
around and around in your head playing messages which tell
what you should and shouldn't do and be. These messages come
from many sources, and a lot of contemporary women hear
stereotypical adages such as:

Women are not as smart as men.
Woman's place is in the home.
Women are to be submissive.
Women should not outrank men.
Women are too emotional to give leadership in high places.
You won't be bored if you really understand how important
housewifery is.
Women are sexually passive.
You are not complete if you are not a mother.

Such messages, or "scripts," lock us into certain roles, bind us to act in certain ways, and sometimes keep us from being whole persons and free spirits. Through the psychology of permission we are unlocked, unbound, and made whole and free, but the language of permission is only meaningful when spoken simply by a significant other (a friend). Affirming messages uttered by the right persons can be life-changers in all kinds of situations. Edith Bunker and women everywhere need to be affirmed and encouraged to develop all their unique gifts to the highest potential.

As a man I have been part of the stifling of women. Maybe now I can be part of the destifilization process by encouraging my fellow human beings. It is sort of like "May I?" the game we played as children, but it is much more significant in real life.

Friend. Edith, you may take ten giant steps.
Edith. May I?
Friend. Yes, you may.

2

It's OK to Be You

The Bunker, Stivic, and Lorenzo families are all playing a new adult game called Group Therapy. (All but Archie, that is, who has concluded that if it is adult it must be dirty; so he has gone to Kelsey's Tavern.) Edith, taking her turn, reads the card she has drawn.

Edith. "Name the person in the world you would like to look like, and tell why." Oh, that's an easy one. Katharine Hepburn.
Gloria. Why, Mom?
Edith. Well, you see her hair and her eyes are a lot like mine. So I don't think Archie would mind too much if I looked like her. And I loved the way she talked in those old movies. Like she was always runnin' out of breath. And she always looked beautiful, no matter. Even when she was supposed to be old and grey.

It is good for Katharine Hepburn to be Katharine Hepburn, but I would like to tell Edith what a beautiful human being she is when Edith is Edith. I say *when* because she is not always allowed or encouraged to be Edith. She is pressed to fit the mold Archie has created for her. This he inadvertently admits when Gloria suggests her mother should be allowed to think for herself.

Archie. Me and your mother think the same. And I know, 'cause I do her thinking for her!

When you are not permitted to have your own thoughts, you feel inferior. If you have any thoughts of your own, you probably will not feel they are worthy of expression. These feelings spawned by Edith's stifling environment cause her also to feel that she is somehow to blame when Archie is not happy.

Archie. What a day this is gonna be. Look at that rain, Edith.

Edith. Oh, I'm sorry, Archie.

Gloria. Daddy, you've got her saying she's sorry like it's her fault it's raining.

Edith's feelings deny her personhood much of the time. Yet at other times (when she is the most beautiful) she is aware of herself and that it is OK to be that self and no one else.

Edith. What you think might mean something to me just like your something might mean nothing to me, only I would never say to you your nothing is nothing 'cause *to you* it's something.

At that moment Edith was more a person than she usually allows herself to be. Taking herself seriously caused Archie to take her seriously, an experience many women in our society seldom have.

"It's OK to be you." "Be aware of self." "Take yourself seriously and expect others to take you seriously." All of these say basically the same thing; yet I want to say it even more strongly to Edith and all women: Love yourself!

You can't really be you if you don't love you. You must love yourself. Jesus said that is necessary if we are to fulfill God's commandment to love our neighbor.

Father John Powell describes this basic human need:

. . . a true and deep love of self, a genuine and joyful self-acceptance, which results in an interior sense of celebration. It's good to be me. I am happy to be me.[1]

As I lead retreats around the country, I usually start by telling people that one of my goals for the weekend will be to enable them to pray meaningfully, "Dear God, I thank you for me." Usually a small group can already say the prayer, but among the rest there are two basic reactions.

One group says, "But isn't it a sin to love yourself? Wasn't the sin of Adam and Everyman the sin of selfishness?" We often confuse self-love and selfishness.

Selfishness is not identical with self-love but its very opposite. Selfishness is one kind of greediness. . . . Greed is a bottomless pit which exhausts the person in an endless effort to satisfy the need without ever reaching satisfaction . . . the selfish person is always anxiously concerned with himself; he is never satisfied, is always restless, always driven by the fear of not getting enough, of missing something, of being deprived of something. He is filled with the burning envy of anyone who might have more . . . this type of person is basically not fond of himself at all, but *deeply dislikes himself... Selfishness is rooted in this very lack of fondness for oneself.* . . . narcissism, like selfishness, is an overcompensation *for the basic lack of self-love.*[2]

Selfishness is our sickness. Self-love is our health.

The second reaction is usually a headshake of disbelief from those who have no sense of their worth or value. They try to convince me that they are completely unlovable, and they believe such an attitude is both righteous and Christian. It is neither. The Good News is that we are loved: You are loved! I am loved!

Without denying the traditional concepts of sin, fallenness, and self-centeredness, we are loved because God is love and because he made us lovable. There is nothing especially Christian about continually putting ourselves down, not if we take seriously the Bible which describes us as being created by God. If a Stradivarius violin is valuable because it was made by Antonio Stradivari or one of his sons, think what our value must be since we are made by God.

But the Bible says even more. After we were created, God declared that "it was good." There is, in addition, even more emphasis on our value if we note the progression of creation in the Genesis 1 story where humanity comes last as the crown of God's creation, the frosting on the cake. This high view of people continues throughout Scripture with God breathing something of himself into us. He made a convenant claiming us as his own people and then in the greatest drama of all time "purchased us with a price" (see 1 Cor. 6:20) by spending his "only begotten Son" Jesus, the Christ.

With that kind of credential, how can we think so little of ourselves? The ancient psalmist was right, "I am wonderfully made" (see Ps. 139:14). So is the contemporary poster-maker who says, "God don't make no junk."

Edith Bunker is unique and wonderfully made. When God created her, he had something fantastic in mind as he does with all human beings, and it is our right and duty to get on with the business of becoming all that he had in mind.

In our church one of the major concerns in church school is the self-esteem of each child. We are convinced they must feel good about who they are if they are going to be God's kind of people, and we try to do everything possible to help them have that sense. One Sunday morning it was beautiful to see those little saints go bounding home wearing special ribbons. They had all been given awards for being something nobody else could be—themselves. The awards were personalized and read: "To Suzie Smith for being the best possible Suzie Smith in the whole world."

Yes, it is OK to be you, Edith Bunker. God planned it that way, and he expects you to be only you, no one else. May God forgive whoever would stifle any human beings in a way that keeps them from experiencing their worth, celebrating their uniqueness, or loving themselves.

3

A Cheaper Cut?

Archie explained to his neighbor, Irene, why women are paid less when doing the same job as men.

Archie. C'mon, Irene, it's a well-known fact that men are worth more than women, an' in the Bible it says "God made man in his own image," he made woman after,—from a rib,—a cheaper cut.

What a terrible way to refer to another human being! More terrible, Archie does not stand alone. He belongs to a long tradition. Aristotle said, "We must look upon the female character as being a sort of natural deficiency," and Tertullian (an early church father) addressed women, "Do you not know that you are Eve? . . . You are the Devil's gateway. How easily you destroyed man, the image of God."

Professor Higgins of *My Fair Lady* added his link to the chain in "Why Can't a Woman Be Like a Man?"

Archie summarizes this traditional view with his favorite name for Edith—Dingbat.

What a terrible way to talk about another human being! One has to ask how can a woman, specifically Edith, stand that kind of dehumanization? The name of the game becomes "cope," and Edith Bunker is one of its champions.

Edith. Oh, I'll never forget the first time I made pot roast for your father. Only he wasn't your father then. We was just keeping company. I

"No matter how mad he says 'dingbat' I always hear a little sweetheart in it."

invited him to my house for dinner and I made him pot roast and that was the first time he ever called me "Dingbat."

Gloria. Well, that's awful, even if he didn't like your cooking.

Edith. Oh, no, he loved it.

Mike. Then why did he call you "Dingbat"?

Edith. Well in them days Archie was too shy to call me sweetheart or darling so instead he called me his "little dingbat." You know what? Ever since then no matter how mad he says "dingbat," I always hear a little sweetheart in it.

Edith gets a gold star for coping, but is that really the game she should be playing? No, there is a more important game. You can call it "life" or "wholeness" or "being human." A person can cope and still lose the game. In our world and down through history a lot of women have coped at the great cost of having much life squeezed out of them, much wholeness denied, and much humanity destroyed.

No wonder so many women not only feel inferior but actually believe in their inferiority and the inferiority of all females when compared to male. Psychological experiments show that this is an almost general affliction. When college women were given identical articles, the only difference being in the author's name, they gave more credibility to the article when the author's name was John T. McKay than when it was Joan T. McKay.[1]

I am concerned about a society that not only treats any human being as inferior but causes a whole segment to think of itself as inferior. Better than coping is the style of women who say you cannot put us down and we are not going to put ourselves down. Women are human beings created in the image of God. Charlotte Holt Clinebell answers the question, What is a woman?

She is a human being, female gender. She is neither as evil nor as holy as Man would make her. She is, like Man, a blend of the good and the evil. If she's in some ways unique, if there are innate differences between the sexes in aptitude or emotions that stem from our biological difference, we don't know yet what they are or the extent of their effect. Whatever our differences, we need to value each other equally, and that means that it must be just as exciting and satisfying in the eyes of our society to Be a Woman! as to be a Man![2]

"We need to value each other equally" is a basic Christian concept that has often been forgotten or denied by those who call themselves Christians. This is hard to understand because Jesus exhibited a concern for the equal value of all persons. Knowing his compassionate attitude toward men, we need to be reminded that not only did he express an equal compassion toward women but he demonstrated and dramatized woman's rightful place. He often went against the custom of his time, having women as his traveling companions and disciples. One of his first evangelists was a woman (the woman at the well in John 4), and the first person to see him after his resurrection was Mary Magdalene. He affirmed another Mary who sat at his feet and listened to his teaching (a man's traditional role), and he rebuked her sister, Martha, for complaining that Mary was not doing her "feminine duty" of serving. He spoke of God as Father; yet in the parable of the lost coin he also compared God's concern for the lost with a woman who has lost her hope for sustenance.

The Apostle Paul got the point and proclaimed, "In Jesus Christ there is neither male nor female. We are one in Christ Jesus" (see Gal. 3:28). Why then is so much done in the name of Christ and the church that is degrading to women? Some have concluded that the entire Bible puts down women. Their case is explained by Gloria's friend.

Sybil. Because the Bible was written by men.
Edith. That's right, Matthew, Mark, Luke . . .
Sybil. Yeah. There wasn't no Patty, Maxine, or Laverne.

More significant is that most biblical interpreters have been men. The few women who sneaked in had to use male sources for most of their learning. Male-dominated interpretation may be the reason for so little emphasis on the female side of God.

When the Bible speaks of God as a he and his fatherhood, we are tempted to see him as exclusively male. How would you react if you heard the preacher address God as "Dear Lord and Mother of Mankind"? What if the choir sang "This Is My Mother's World"? Before you become too indignant, you should know there is a biblical base for attributing feminine characteristics to God.

Many Old Testament words which describe God and the actions of God are in the feminine gender. Isaiah 66:13 counterbalances the male Father-God concept: "As a mother comforts her child so will I [God speaking] comfort you." This God, the holy one about whom we can speak only by giving him humanlike attributes, is described as acting like a woman, a mother. What good news! It affirms a side of life that our society is in danger of losing and gives a new wholeness to our concept of God.

Jungian psychologists tell us that individual personalities are made up of two components, the male and the female. Irene Claremont de Castillejo describes these in *Knowing Woman:*

If we realize that on the whole the basic masculine attitude to life is that of focus, division and change; and the feminine (in either sex) is more nearly an attitude of acceptance, an awareness of the unity of life and a readiness for relationship, then we can accept a rough division of the psyche into masculine and feminine.*[3]

This same division is explained by John Powell:

Male	*Female*
The male component or sexual function of the soul engages predominantly in things of the *head and the will:*	The female component is associated with things of the *heart:* the appreciation of
order	art
logic	music
power	religion
courage	nature
protection	flowers
dependability	

What a gray world it would be if only the male component were emphasized, what gray people and what a gray God; a world, people and a God of order, logic, power, etc., but no heart. Yet that is the danger in thinking of God as only "he" or in suggesting that men or the masculine components are superior leaving us a society where people at best are hardware.

If wholeness is our goal, we must balance and harmonize the male and female components without negating either in any

"As a mother comforts her child so will I comfort you."

person. Knowing God as male and female may be the starting place. The Father-God concept by itself is inadequate. Who wants a God without a heart? Could this be the meaning of the doctrine of the Holy Spirit? A number of theologians have thought of the Trinity as family: Father, Son, and Holy Spirit equal Father, Child and Mother. It is to help us to understand the feminine side. The fruit of the spirit is heart fruit, feminine fruit: love, joy, peace, patience, kindness, goodness, faithfulness, gentleness, and self-control. I guess I would chalk "self-control" up to the male side! Add that to the masculine God that is more often emphasized, and we discover a wholeness that not only inspires but provides a model for the wholeness we all seek.

Once I know God as male and female, I, as a male, am free to acknowledge the female (the things of the heart) in me. This not only brings my own growth but enables me to encourage others to awaken and develop their dormant components. At the same time we continue to accept and affirm the male components.

Maleness and femaleness are necessary for a whole human being and for an adequate understanding of God. In a healthy society the Archie Bunkers will be secure enough in their masculinity to freely discover their feminine side and where women can cultivate their masculine side without any fear of sacrificing femininity.

A healthy society will allow and encourage each woman, including Edith Bunker, to be the woman she is, to claim for herself the equality that is her God-given right. But women should be careful not to get caught in the trap of using men as their standard thereby suppressing their femaleness that our society so greatly needs. Our world needs Edith with all her love, gentleness, grace, and sensitivity, and none of these qualities should be stifled in her.

At the same time the masculine side in Edith that has been stifled must be encouraged. Someone has said that Edith Bunker is all heart. That is only half right. There is another side to her that is rational, logical, orderly, and so on, and that side needs to be enabled and nurtured so she can become what God intended her to be—a whole person with both head and heart, a woman person.

4

The Sea of
Matrimony

"The sea of matrimony" is an expression I have heard ever since I can remember. I had thought of it as an acceptable phrase until I heard Archie Bunker talk to Mike.

Archie. Listen, Meathead, when you been in the raging sea of matrimony as long as me, you'll learn that the husband is the captain of the ship and the wife is the deckhand. And when the captain says, "Shove off," the deckhand shoves.

There is a sense in which this un-Christian concept of marriage works.

Amelia. (Edith's friend) Of all the people I know, you're practically the only one who has a happy marriage.
Edith. Really? Me and Archie . . . Oh, thank you.
Amelia. What is your secret, Edith?
Edith. Oh, I ain't got no secret. Archie and me still have our fights. Of course we don't let them go on too long. Somebody always says "I'm sorry." And Archie always says, "It's okay, Edith."

Yes, it works. They stay together and "keep the peace" but at tremendous cost to Edith's person, peace, and esteem.

The crime is that this marriage is not unusual. The captain-deckhand relationship is just one more version of an increasing

"The raging sea of matrimony."

number of marriage philosophies based on a one up-one down mentality. (Interestingly, the one up is always the man, and the one down is always the woman).

This mentality is manifest in many forms and phrases, most of which have little to do with marriage and are about as romantic as a dish rag. The vocabulary is usually more like one would hear in a school for delinquent boys, obedience schools for untrained dogs, the court's ancient monarchies, or board rooms of modern corporations. The words and concepts are degrading to the biblical idea of marriage and to the *beauty* of marriage experienced by some couples.

It is just not beautiful to hear an accountant tell how to live in a marriage by the numbers and speak of a "chain of command" as in the case of one nationally prominant marriage and family workshop. It is just as offensive to put down woman by preaching *submission, subordination,* and *obedience,* especially if these words are neatly joined under the umbrella of "God's order."

I am greatly concerned about the destructive things which happen to so many persons who have bought into this hierarchical concept. I am a little baffled by its popularity as expressed in that manual of marital manipulation entitled *The Total Woman* by Marabel Morgan.

Ms. Morgan has a high goal, "I didn't want a marginal marriage. I wanted the best,"[1] and she seems sincere. But can she be sincerely wrong? Yes, I believe so. Marriage is a meaningful relationship, and people in good relationship do not need to dehumanize each other with little tricks in order to have their own way or to get things they want. In Ms. Morgan's case this includes new refrigerators, interior decoration, and vacations.

Meaningful marital relationships do not have room for such statements as:

God planned for woman to be under her husband's *rule* (italics mine).
. . . if there is a difference of opinion, the king makes the decision.

. . . What if the king makes a wrong decision? . . . The queen is still to follow him forthwith.

Treat him like a king and cater to his needs.

Graciously adapt to his way, even if you know it's wrong.

Allowing your husband to be your family president is just good business.[2]

And so the book goes, with a lot of "roles" and "pigeon holes" thrown in. There must be a better way.

There is a better way, and it doesn't include words like *king, captain, obedience, submission, chain of command, divine order.* The better way uses one significant word: *partner.*

The *American Heritage Dictionary* defines *partner* as "a person associated with another in some activity of common interest." It goes on, "Partner implies a relationship frequently between two people, in which each has equal status and a certain independence but also implicit or formal obligations to the other or others." Person, relationship, equal status, independence and obligation are much better terms.

What does it mean to be a partner in marriage? The dictionary says a person is "a living human being especially as distinguished from an animal or a thing." Some married folks don't make that distinction; they treat their mates as animals and things. When Archie says "stay" or "stifle," he is treating Edith like a pet dog. When he walks in the house at night and bellows, "Edith, where is my beer?" he is treating her like a thing, a dispensing machine. In both cases he kills any chance of partnership because he fails to see and acknowledge Edith as a person. I am sure if she honestly dared to verbalize her feelings she would say what I have heard many others say of their failing marriage, "He [or she] makes me feel like I am less than a person."

If we are looking for a biblical basis for marriage, let us note that Jesus was *person* oriented. Many of those with whom he came in contact had for one reason or another been made to feel they were less than persons. Jesus restored their personhood. Zacchaeus was a crook up a tree when Jesus befriended him.

This not only got Zacchaeus down from the tree with astonishing speed, but, more importantly, it enabled him to become an honest person.

Simon was a bowl of gelatin who wanted to be a rock; so Jesus started loving him and calling him *Rock*. Simon became the person he wanted to be, causing everybody to call him Rock (see Luke 19:1–10).

Likewise, the woman caught in adultery must have felt like a "thing" until Jesus expressed his forgiveness and sent her away a person encouraged to sin no more.

Even at his execution, Jesus recognized a person, hanging on the cross next to him. Everybody else saw only a thief, but Jesus promised that person eternal life.

Personhood is what Jesus was about, and that is what our marriages must also be about. Marriage is partnership, and partnership is a person-to-person relationship in which, as Carl Rogers says,

I can come to prize myself as the richly varied person I am. Perhaps I can openly *be* more of this person. . . . Possibly then I can be a *real* member of a partnership, because I am on the road to being a real person. And I am hopeful that I can encourage my partner to follow his or her own road to a unique personhood, which I would love to share.[3]

The relationship of love is that undefinable word about which volumes have been written; yet we have no definition. The attempts help, for at least they give clues. The one that helps me most is Dr. Harry Stack Sullivan's: "When the satisfaction, security and development of another person becomes as significant to you as your own satisfaction, security and development, love exists."[4]

I know of no better definition, but I do know a better description —the crucifix. Every time I see one, I hear, "God loves like that." I cannot attain such love, but it shows me the direction in which to reach, and it colors all my relationships, especially the relationship with my partner in marriage.

Paul's statement in Galatians 3:28 should be a strong enough injunction for Christians to give equal status to all, especially their marriage partners. But some of Paul's other statements about women and marriage confuse the issue. "Wives, be subject to your husbands, as to the Lord. For the husband is the head of the wife" (Eph. 5:22–23, RSV). "Let a woman learn in silence with all submissiveness. I permit no woman to teach or to have authority over men; she is to keep silent" (1 Tim. 2:11–12, RSV).

When we look at the example of Jesus and at Galatians 3:28, it is difficult to know what to do with the words from 1 Timothy and Ephesians unless we use some basic principles of biblical interpretation. Biblical interpretation is a complicated science which I hope not to oversimplify by suggesting three principles. *What Are The Surrounding Materials?* If we continue to read the Ephesians passage we find that Paul also gives instructions for slaves and masters, affirming the practice of slavery. We do not, however, because of other Biblical emphasis accept slavery, making these instructions invalid. If we find these instructions invalid can we not also question the validity of verses 22 and 23 which imply another form of slavery?

The Length of the Future Other Scriptures show us that the New Testament church and Paul seemed to believe that they were living in the "end-times" and the return of Christ was imminent. Thus Paul's instructions were interim rather than long-range. In other words, if Paul could have anticipated the world lasting another 2,000 years, many of his instructions would probably have been different.

The Cultural This principle gives consideration to what was going on in the culture of Paul's time such as education of women, and cultural Jewish practices which would undoubtedly influence Paul's thinking and necessitate practices which would not be necessary in another culture.

We must also keep in mind that Paul was human, and like all humans, he was "in process." Time and growth would be necessary for him to know the total implication of his Galatian statement. We have had two thousand years, and we still don't know

"Partners in marriage."

fully or practice the truth that "in Jesus Christ there is neither male nor female." The whole New Testament, however, proclaims equal status. Charlotte Clinebell describes it as meeting in the middle:

> The "middle" is the place where both men and women can get their needs met, individually and together, without one sex on the top and the other on the bottom. In the middle we can love and work together. I am saying to men, "Meet me in the middle! I am no longer willing to meet you anywhere else. I want to share the excitement and joy of life with you, but I am not willing to be 'one down.' I need to meet you in the middle to be fully human—or to be and do whatever is possible for me. You need to meet me in the middle for the same reason."[5]

I prefer the word *commitment* to *obligation.* Commitment creates interdependence which when added to independence creates the tension necessary for the growth and development of the individuals and the relationship. The marriage of historians Will and Ariel Durant is a beautiful example. Whey they were married, she was fifteen years old and came to the wedding on roller skates. Many said the marriage would never last. Since that was over sixty years ago, it looks like the critics were wrong. Writer Jim Bishop visited them on their golden anniversary, and he says that when they fell in love they forgot the use of the personal pronoun. All of "his" books "we" wrote. Yet deleting the personal pronoun included no sacrifice of independence for either. Bishop saw them as two trees growing side by side, two grand, beautiful oaks, growing side by side. But he also noted that beneath the ground their roots have become intertwined and have become one.

It is the beauty of that relationship and the contributions of those two individual lives that convince me that it is OK to be *partners* in marriage.

Edith has been faithful in her marriage but too often at the cost of her own individuality. Interestingly enough, Archie is cheating himself. When he stifles Edith he stifles the quality of their marriage.

Edith somewhere must have a dream of a partnership where there is a oneness that contributes to the whole of the individuals involved. I think I saw that dream in her eyes the night she heard Mike read these words of Gibran at a friend's wedding.

> You were born together, and together you
>   shall be forevermore.
> You shall be together when the white
>   wings of death scatter your days.
> Ay, you shall be together even in the
>   silent memory of God.
> But let there be spaces in your togetherness,
> And let the winds of the heavens dance
>   between you.
>
> Love one another, but make not a bond
>   of love:
> Let it rather be a moving sea between
>   the shores of your souls.
> Fill each other's cup but drink not from
>   one cup.
> Give one another of your bread but eat
>   not from the same loaf.
> Sing and dance together and be joyous,
>   but let each one of you be alone,
> Even as the strings of a lute are alone
>   though they quiver with the same music.
>
> Give your hearts, but not into each
>   other's keeping.
> For only the hand of Life can contain
>   your hearts.
> And stand together yet not too near
>   together:
> For the pillars of the temple stand apart,
> And the oak tree and the cypress grow
>   not in each other's shadow.[6]

"Partners in marriage."

5

What Price Success?

Now that Gloria, her daughter, has been raised and is married and gone (moved from the Bunker house to the one next door), Edith has become a Sunshine Lady. Once a week she goes to a home for the aged to bring "hope to the hopeless" and "cheer to the cheerless." She looks forward to that special day each week because as she says, "It gives me a purpose in life."

Archie. You always had a purpose. You are my what?
Edith. Wife.
Archie. And we live in a what?
Edith. House.
Archie. Now put them two together and what have you got?
Edith. Wife house?
Archie. No, house wife, Edith! That is your purpose in life—to feed and care for your husband! . . . And if you like charity work, Edith, just remember what Charlotte Heston said in the *Ten Commandments,* "Charity begins at home." You got plenty to do right here.
Edith. But I ain't. You go to work and Gloria and Mike go to work and that leaves me alone with nothing to do all day and nothing to look forward to.

Edith is articulating a feeling that many married women in our society experience sooner or later; they feel they have reached a dead-end. Most women I talk to who feel this way have given housewifery their best shot. They have played the role of happy housewife-heroine according to the grocery store wo-

"The Sunshine Lady."

men's magazines which they have read with the fervor of a Bible student. They have listened to the TV commercials, clipped and saved all the coupons, and sat at the feet of the high priestess of all happy housewife-heroines—Heloise. All of this is simply the modern version of the older rural idea that a fulfilled woman is basically a homebody who makes a lot of babies and a lot of bread.

Archie says it a little differently: "Women was created for two things, making meals and babies."

I don't agree with Archie, but maybe there was a time when women could be convinced that that was all they were created for. No longer. We not only have an excess of babies, but freezers, transportation, and the supermarkets make bread easily accessible. Other conveniences continue to widen the gap between necessary work and the "decoupage syndrome." One woman concludes:

> Housekeeping is a task that swells to fill every moment a woman will give to it. Each woman has to decide where to cut it off. For years I turned the collars and cuffs on all my husband's shirts and almost doubled their wear that way. Fortunately shirts are now made so that their collars cannot be turned. I was a diehard about ironing pillowcases, but I finally gave it up as a vice . . .
>
> Much of what passes for homemaking in our culture is monkey business. I made that decision after a few years of dutifully doing things like decorating soap with decals and copying useless recipes and reading most of the advertisements that came in the mail.[1]

Why is this responsible woman who is also a mother and wife saying what I (as a man) would be afraid to say? Because she has wrestled with what it means to be a fulfilled person, and housewife in itself is not fulfilling her. I don't think she is saying that housewifery and mothering are unimportant. It is just that they are not all of one's life, and neither are they of such scope that one should build an entire existence, fulfillment, and identity upon them. Why?

"Women was created for two things, making meals and babies."

In the first place, parenting is not a one-person job. Children need nurturing input from all kinds of human beings. They received this when the extended family was intact. Children were in touch with and raised by mom, dad, brother, sister, cousin, aunt, uncle, grandma, and grandad. Most children now are not so privileged. Mom and dad often live hundreds or thousands of miles away from the rest of the family. This may occur because the father is furthering his education, or his job may have necessitated not only one move, but many. Often men in our society become so "commited" to education or a new job that they leave the mother and child to live in virtual isolation.

A mother should not be expected to spend all her time in a child's world, and certainly the child needs more human contact than one adult. The father needs to take seriously his responsibility as a nurturing parent. The excuse that he is busy "earning bread" for his family is not acceptable. Children can get by with much less of the plastic bread we provide these days. They need more of us as nurturing parents.

In addition the child needs contact with other adults and children such as can be found at nursery school, daycare centers, playgrounds, and churches. Of course, there needs to be a balance. A child should not spend all waking hours at the daycare center which often happens with children of working mothers. We need to correct this by acknowledging that there is nothing sacred about an eight-hour work day. Industry and business must make it possible for individuals to work two, four, or six hours a day. It is high time the company adjust to the needs of parents and children. Families and wives have been adjusting to business long enough.

The life expectancy of the average American woman is around seventy-five years. This means that many married women still have forty years to live after their children are in grade school and twenty-five or thirty years after they graduate from high school. What does the traditional woman do that last thirty years? In some cases she vegetates; in others she continues to "mother" her adult children and their spouses in an attempt to overcome her feelings of worthlessness and uselessness. Healthy women find other purposes to which they commit themselves before those years arrive; they prepare and plan for the great opportunity that the empty nest allows.

Because the high cost of living makes it necessary for many women to work, nearly half of all women between the ages of eighteen and sixty-four are employed outside the home. Wives and mothers have to find a balance among work, parenting, and housewifery, but many women are inhibited by guilt placed on them by those who preach that a woman must be a full-time homebody.

Many housewifery tasks border on meaninglessness. How can we expect people to build their lives upon being the head janitor? Vacuuming and dusting are just that, and people who get a kick out of emptying the garbage need their heads examined. I know the Brother Lawrence concept of doing it to the "glory of God"; so I say OK, empty the garbage to the glory of God, but don't take too long. There are more important things to do to the glory of God in our world. Let's share in the meaningless, menial tasks so that we can all do the more fulfilling tasks.

God has given each of us special gifts, and our responsibility is to discern our individual gifts and to use them for service to humanity and for the glory of God. However, discerning personal gifts is a useless exercise for many women because our society allows so few opportunities for those gifts to be used. In fact, a kind of programming even inhibits the process of discernment.

They grow up watching women on television whose main problems are how to get their wash whiter and floors shinier and to make themselves more beautiful and to smell better and to attract or retain a husband. Children read textbooks that hardly ever mention women, and when they do, emphasize women in a domestic capacity; after all Betsy Ross is famous for her sewing. Children see ads that use women for specific physical traits, and hear endless jokes about the ineptitude and failings of women.[2]

As a result, society cheats itself out of some of the very people it needs. Many problems could be solved by some bright minds that have in the past known their highest challenge to be one more way to fix hamburger. Many problems need a kind, mothering concern and sensitivity. Those who are and have been mothers can do that kind of caring. Wars and competition have hardened society's heart. When wise mothers become a part of our think-tanks and our decision-making process, maybe our collective heart will again be tenderized.

Well, we are way into the chapter on who is a successful person, and we haven't yet used the word *success.* I am a little afraid of the word, for I have seen its intoxicating power destroy the lives and relationships of some beautiful human beings. I would not want to turn Edith into a Vince Lombardi with his "winning isn't everything, it's the only thing" philosophy, but neither would I want her to avoid success or worse yet fear it.

The work of Dr. Matina Horner, president of Radcliffe College and a psychology professor, is well known. Her psychological studies with college women show that many of them are anxiety-ridden over the prospect of success; they experience anxious conflict over what might happen should they should succeed or excel in certain areas. Some degree of concern on their part seems legitimate; Dr. Matina feels that negative attitudes toward successful women have increased since the mid-sixties.[3]

Edith can understand this syndrome. Archie is not only jealous of her volunteer work, but when she starts getting paid, he becomes threatened by her success. If Edith does a job that she doesn't get paid for, it is not worth anything. If she gets paid for it, that is a sign of success, and success is only for men. Because Edith lives with that kind of thinking, I want to assure her there is nothing wrong in being successful. She doesn't have to fear it or avoid it.

I am still a little wary about the word *success.* I want to be sure that it is understood in the context of fulfillment and responsibility. Harry Stack Sullivan said, "Most people are caricatures of the persons they might have been.[4] I don't think Edith has to be a "might have been." She and all humans must be encouraged to be all they were intended to be, but many women have been victims of stereotyping, and they need to know they are capable of infinitely wide responsibilities. The Bible not only declares this capability but affirms the woman who lives to its capacity:

> A good wife who can find?
> She does him good, and not harm,
>   all the days of her life.
> She seeks wool and flax,
>   and works with willing hands.
> She is like the ships of the merchant,
>   she brings her food from afar.
> She rises while it is yet night
>   and provides food for her household
>   and tasks for her maidens.
> She considers a field and buys it;
>   with the fruit of her hands she plants a vineyard.
> She girds her loins with strength
>   and makes her arms strong.
> She perceives that her merchandise is profitable.
>   Her lamp does not go out at night.
> She puts her hands to the distaff,
>   and her hands hold the spinkle.
> She opens her hand to the poor,
>   and reaches out her hands to the needy.
> She is not afraid of snow for her household,
>   for all her household are clothed in scarlet.
> She makes herself coverings;
>   her clothing is fine linen and purple.
> Her husband is known in the gates,
>   when he sits among the elders of the land.
> She makes linen garments and sells them;
>   she delivers girdles to the merchant.
> Strength and dignity are her clothing,
>   and she laughs at the time to come.

She opens her mouth with wisdom,
and the teaching of kindness is on her tongue (Prov. 31:10, 12–26,
RSV).

How is that for a resumé—manager, provider, employer, investor, buyer, philanthropist, teacher? Could there be any company president that would not want to employ such a person? Yes, one who might be afraid such a well-qualified person would take his job.

6

People Smart

Gloria. A father and his son are driving along in a car and the car crashes. And the father is killed.

Edith. Oh, that's sad.

Archie. It's only a story, Edith.

Gloria. Anyway, the father is killed and the son is badly injured, so they rush him to the hospital and take him into the operating room. The surgeon comes in, takes one look at the boy, and says, "I can't operate on that boy—he's my son!" How come?

The above dialogue occurred at the beginning of an "All in the Family" episode. It took the rest of the program for anybody to guess the answer. Mike guessed that the father was a priest, a Catholic father. Archie guessed, "The kid on the operating table was his own double!" His friend Barney guessed, "It's like in them weirdo movies where the dead guy transports himself outta his corpse!"

Three strikes and the men were out. Then Edith spoke, "I think I know the answer, Archie. I figured it out doing the beds. The surgeon couldn't do the operation because she was the boy's mother." Edith is not stupid; she is not a dingbat. She is a wise woman who, like many women, has had to stifle herself intellectually in order to prop up her husband's superiority feelings. In this case Archie protected himself and negated Edith by claiming, "The riddle was made up by a woman. The answer's got a make-believe woman doctor in it. And I ain't surprised you got it, Edith, 'cause it's a woman's riddle . . . and I don't wanna hear no more about it."

Edith slipped up. She forgot that she is even supposed to stifle her thinking. Try as she may, her wisdom still seeps through.

The dictionary defines *wisdom* as "understanding what is true, right, or lasting."

In "Song of the Open Road," Walt Whitman said it another way:

> Wisdom is not finally tested in the schools,
> Wisdom cannot be passed on from one having
>   it to one not having it.
> Wisdom is of the soul, is not susceptible
>   of proof, is its own proof.

I never realized how Edith fit the definitions above and how wise she really is or how wise she has to be until I read the words of Pope Xystus I in *The Ring:* "The chief aim of wisdom is to enable one to bear with the stupidity of the ignorant." The application is obvious. In this context, here is some of the "Wit and Wisdom of Edith Bunker" (I had to add the word *wit* because I am not sure you can have wisdom without it).

Edith explains wisdom when she responds to Gloria's concern about not being smart enough for Michael:

Edith. Oh, Gloria, you should never say that. There's all kinds of smart. There's book smart and there's people smart. And sometimes people smart is more important.

Wisdom is "people smart."

Marriage counseling:

Following the birth of Joey, Gloria finds that some of her feelings toward Mike have changed, especially her sexual feelings. She consults her mother:

Gloria. Ma, was there ever a time when you had no feelings toward Daddy?
Edith. Yes, there was times when I put myself on the shelf, too . . . But that didn't mean I didn't love Archie, cause marriage is more than just two

people turning out the lights and not going to sleep. Gloria, there are two men in your life now—a little one and a big one. And they both need attention. You gotta spend more time talking to Mike, taking walks with him. Go to movies with him . . . and pretty soon you'll be surprised what else you'll be doing with him.

The obvious:

Gloria. **(after being fired from her job)** Maybe I went to the water cooler too often or to the ladies room too much.
Edith. If you did one, they can't blame you for doing the other.

Inspiration:

Edith. Maybe God put unhappiness in the world so when we get to heaven we can notice the improvement.

Theology:

Archie. It ain't funny. Our grandson's layin' there covered with original sin, and if he don't get baptized, he ain't going to heaven!
Edith. I don't worry about Joey. He's an innocent little baby, and God made him beautiful so he must love him. And God ain't gonna hold it against him just because he ain't been sprinkled.

Fighting:

Edith. Family quarrels is like a hole in a sock. If you don't patch 'em up, they get bigger and bigger and pretty soon you got more hole than sock.

Worry:

Edith. I worry more about Archie getting worried . . . cause he don't know how to worry without getting upset.

Reality:
Edith is saddened by the news of Gloria's moving.

Gloria. Oh, Ma, you knew I'd be moving sometime.
Edith. Oh, yeah, but sometimes sometime comes too soon!

Logic:
When Edith realizes that Archie is being conned by the representative from the "Home Energy Conservation Program" (he sells aluminum siding), she responds to Archie's "he ain't selling nothing" with "How can he make a living selling nothing?"

Trouble:

Edith. Poor Archie! Two big problems at once. That's the trouble with trouble—it always comes in twos and threes. Not like happy things. They only come one at a time. Or not at all.

Compassion:
Edith knows that true wisdom is a matter of both the head and the heart.

Edith. (in response to Gloria's question about abortion) Well, when I watch them women talkin' about it on TV, I guess it's yes—but when I'm sittin' here talkin' to my own daughter who's carrying my own grandchild . . . Oh, Gloria, I'm already in love with the baby.

In most societies there has been some wise person who would act as an arbitrator in settling arguments between differing individuals. This was part of the function of the judges in the Old Testament as well as the function of people of higher rank such as King Solomon. The wisest sages are not philosophers spewing syllogisms but simple storytellers who help people see the truth. Edith is a storyteller-arbitrator. When Gloria and Mike had the worst disagreement of their marriage, one that got out of control with no peaceful conclusion in sight, Edith showed a beautiful and caring assertiveness to get them to listen.

Then she told her story:

Edith. When I was a little girl, my mother and father got into a terrible fight, that started just because there wasn't enough maple syrup for my father's pancakes.

Mike. Ma, what we're arguing about here is a lot more important than maple syrup.

Edith. Now wait a minute, I ain't finished. They didn't talk to each other for three weeks. Even after they made up, things was never really the same between them. So, before you start sayin' things to each other that you can never take back, you better stop now and think about how much you really mean to each other. Now, I know maple syrup is a little thing, but would you feel any better breakin' apart over something bigger?

Gloria and Michael then made up. We could continue quoting Edith, but the point is made. She is a wise woman, and with little encouragement. If she were ever affirmed, think of the benefits that could be gained by those around her.

Edith helps us begin to understand why H. L. Mencken refers to women as "the Realists of the Race":

Women decide the larger question of life correctly and quickly, not because they are lucky guessers, not because they are divinely inspired, not because they practice magic inherited from savagery, but simply and solely because they have sense. They see at a glance what most men cannot see with searchlights and telescopes; they are at grips with the essentials of a problem before men have finished debating its mere externals. They are the supreme realists of the race. Apparently illogical, they are the possessors of a rare and subtle super-logic. Apparently whimsical, they hang to the truth with a tenacity which carries them through every phase of its incessant, jelly-like shifting of form.[1]

I don't know if I agree that the line can be drawn so straight or so clearly between women and men. Neither do I want to put down men in order to elevate women. But I know in my head and I feel in my bones that an ingredient is missing from our society. It started just as a feeling one day when my wife, Doris, recounted her experience on a panel in trying to talk with a male governmental bureaucrat about the rights of the consumer. Not only was he not hearing her, but he acted as if he thought it impossible that a woman might have anything valid to say. He did not even try to tune in to her wave length that reflected people and their lives, health, and rights. He spoke only of things—hardware, numbers, and profits. Even though he and his department have since been forced to listen because of Doris's zeal and the concern of others like her, at that time the best he could do was to give her a condescending verbal pat on the head and say, "There is just so much you don't understand."

It was then that I knew he was wrong. Actually, it was vice versa; there was so much he didn't understand. Oh, I am sure he knew a lot, but like many of us men, his knowledge far exceeded his understanding. Because our society is primarily run by men, there is a lack of basic sensitive understanding, the kind that many women seem to have.

As I look at my personal growth, I believe I am gaining sensitive understanding as part of my life-style. At least, I hope I am, but where is it coming from? I'm learning it from women. Women have helped me understand that consumers are people, that we must become ecologically responsible, and that there is a better way to eat that will give me health and at the same time help solve the world hunger problems.

Sensitive understanding is really a general heading under which you could place the spunky intelligence of a Karen Horney, the concern to put the mother back into nature of a Rachel Carson, the saintliness of a Jane Addams, the selflessness of an Anne Sullivan, the intercultural understanding of a Pearl Buck, the good sense of a Margaret Mead, the "generosity of spirit" of an Eleanor Roosevelt, and the people politics of a Barbara Jordan.

"Sensitive understanding."

Many more wise women are today waiting or, in many cases, struggling for opportunity to sit in places of leadership where they can make the difference that can lead to the renewal of our nation, its institutions, and its people. All they need is the opportunity.

Still Afraid to Ask

When Mike complains to Gloria that she is sexually rejecting him for the baby, Joey, she decides to talk to her mother. She is a little surprised to discover her mother understands.

Gloria. Then you know what I mean?
Edith. Oh, yea . . . when you was a baby, I had the same problem, but I couldn't talk to my mother. In those days, we didn't even have books like *Everything You Always Wanted to Know about* (uh) *But Was Afraid to Ask."*
Gloria. Did you read that book?
Edith. Oh, no.
Gloria. So you still don't know everything?
Edith. No, and I'm still afraid to ask.

This little dialogue tells at least two things about Edith: (1) Sex is a word which for reasons of embarrassment, conditioning, and "morality" she cannot say. A number of other words come under the same heading. (2) She's rather ignorant about this subject which effects so much of her life. Archie is pretty much in the same boat. He not only feels that sex and related words should only be spoken at the tavern, but he is also against using words that refer to human reproduction:

Archie (to Gloria). No, get away! You ain't supposed to be carryin' nothin' in your condition!
Gloria. Daddy, don't say "condition." It sounds like I've got the heartbreak of psoriasis. I don't have a condition, I'm pregnant!

Archie. Don't say that! Can't you say "expectant"?

Edith. When I was a little girl, and a woman was startin' to show, we used to say she was expectin' a bundle from heaven—but everybody knew it was really a baby.

Archie. Well, I'd like to get back to them days. A little class wouldn't hurt the world. Hereinafter, when we discuss Gloria, we'll say she's expectin'!

Edith. Or "in the family way."

Archie. Or "with child."

I agree a little class wouldn't hurt the world, but what is so classy about saying "expectin' " rather than "pregnant," and why can't we talk about sex some place besides the tavern?

I am not sure Archie would answer such questions, but if he would, I think whatever he said would add up to a bottom line that says, "Sex is nasty."

These attitudes inhibit Archie and Edith as married persons. Thus the reason for Edith's response when her cousin who is disappointed in her own marriage asks Edith:

Amelia. When in bed with Archie, do you see pinwheels and skyrockets and fire works like the Fourth of July?

Edith. No, with me and Archie it is more like Thanksgiving.

Such attitudes and experiences are typical of a large segment of our population. If we are to know the quality of sexual wholeness God intended for us, some affirmations need to be incorporated into our lives.

Our sexuality is God's good idea. First, the Bible says we were made by God in his image. Second, he made us male and female. Third, what and how he made us was good—not nasty, not dirty, not bad, but *good.*

Why then do so many Christian people act otherwise? Why do they think that Christianity and the biblical view are both antisexual? Part of the reason is poor biblical interpretation. For example, I have heard people suggest that there was something bad about their bodies and that is why Adam and Eve had to make aprons to cover themselves. Not so. Making aprons was motivated by the desire to hide from each other because of their self-consciousness, a byproduct of their self-centered attitudes which caused "the fall." Their prefall condition was one of good nakedness: "And the man and his wife were both naked, and were not ashamed" (Gen. 2:25, RSV).

Throughout Scripture this "not ashamed" attitude toward the body is maintained. The mark of the covenant (circumcision) is placed on the male organ, and the covenant blessing is passed on by the recipient of the blessing laying his hand on the genitals of the giver of the blessing. (Translators seem to have a hard time saying "genitals." The closest they dare come is "thigh" which is the word they use as a substitute).

In the New Testament the word *body* becomes a spiritual metaphor when the church is referred to as "the body of Christ." In Ephesians 5:26–27 the church image is nude, in the husband-wife context. Her body is "washed and without spot, wrinkle, or blemish."

Our bodies are good. They were created by God, and we are not to be ashamed of them.

Sexual response is a natural body function (like breathing, salivating, and blinking the eyes). Just this simple fact is liberating to me. A few years ago I learned that anger is a basic human emotion; just as we are sometimes happy or sad, it is natural to be angry at times. I had been denying my anger, but when I realized that anger is a legitimate feeling, I could admit my rage without destroying my self-image. Then I began to learn how to channel my anger appropriately, and in the process I am becoming a healthier, happier person.

Realizing that the sexual response is a natural function enables me not to be guilty about my sexuality. Instead I can be thankful for it and in gratitude discover not only its function but its benefits.

Sex is pleasure. One of the good things happening in our day is that words like *pleasure, joy,* and *fun* are being asociated with sex. Masters and Johnson's *The Pleasure Bond* and Alex Comfort's *The Joy of Sex* are two examples. One would think that everyone knows sex is pleasure, but many do not. Some women, for instance, have been conditioned to think that sex is a burden they must endure. And there are men for whom sex is work. They are so accustomed to believing that the man must produce that they end up even working at sex, and they miss the joy.

Sex is not a burden or work but play in its highest form. A large segment of the church has viewed the sex act as being only for procreation, and this has hindered the pleasure concept. We must reemphasize that sex is also for re-creation. It is that high form of play that *recreates* the initial commitment, oneness, and fulfillment that a man and woman in love can experience and know again and again on an ascending scale.

Sex can and should be talked about. There are private, sacred aspects about sex, and an appropriate intimacy must always be maintained. Discussing one's own sexual experience is necessarily limited with respect to the individuals involved; yet, in general, husbands and wives seldom discuss their sex lives with each other. Often married couples come to me for counseling because their marriage is dying and they are not responding to each other sexually. The scenario goes something like this:

She says: "Well, if you just wouldn't touch me in such-and-such a place [it might be any one of many places on her body, but for the sake of this example, let's say the left elbow]."

Well, this is news to him. In fact, he always thought she kind of liked the left-elbow business. Whenever they started making love, he went for the left elbow, not aware he was turning her off. So he says, "Why didn't you tell me?" Good question. Why didn't she tell him? She answers, "You never asked." Good answer. He should have asked. Both have been irresponsible to themselves and to each other in never talking about their sex lives. Had they verbalized their feelings about their likes, dislikes, and sexual desires and needs, their marriage and their sex life might have been different.

In premarital counseling, I encourage couples to set aside times to talk clinically about their sex lives. I say "clinically" because I think they should deal with specifics as observed, felt, and desired, and they should ask why when their feelings differ. In this way they can grow in self-understanding and develop a better understanding of the other person.

Love making is an art and should not be inhibited by any standards other than those of the artists themselves. It is too bad that phrases like "unnatural acts" or "abnormal sex life" are used in referring to what a couple does together. Husbands and wives should be free to experiment and enjoy each other with a mutual concern.

They should not be inhibited by trying to hold to some kind of culturally inflicted norm whether it be a Kinsey statistic as to how many times the average couple has intercourse per week or a cultic myth that the missionary position is the only position.

Love making takes time. The word *time* is significant when discussing sex. Couples not only need to know the best time for each person, but they also need to give priority to taking enough time for love making. Often couples only receive from each other the leftover portion of the day—not necessarily the best time for love making. It is important for couples to block out regular periods of time to be alone and and to be together, including "mini-honeymoons." Such a time commitment will do wonders for both the marriage and the individuals. But what about the children? When Doris and I return from one of our mini-honeymoons, we are always glad to note that our daughters have benefitted, rather than suffered, by being away from us for a couple of days.

Educate yourself sexually. Most of us don't know very much about sex, and much of what we do know is based on fiction rather than fact. Most of the so-called sex education classes we took during school years would have better been named "reproduction classes." About all we learned was how to have and not have babies, plus a few warnings about venereal disease. As a married person I need *sex* education. I want to know more about my wife's body and my own so that we can both have more joy. Reading good books and taking classes can be helpful. *The Pleasure Bond* by Masters and Johnson is an excellent source of information. It disposes of some old wives' tales as well as discussing the emotional and relational aspects of marital sex.

Sexual self-esteem, capability, and potential are enhanced by knowledge and understanding. Masters and Johnson indicate that women have a much higher potential for sexual pleasure than previously thought, and it is probably higher than male capacity. I think Edith is gaining this awareness. In fact, I have a feeling that Edith may have taken a peek at *The Pleasure Bond* in some dark corner of the library because she is learning some new things about herself. The way her esteem is growing is illustrated by the way she deals with Archie's response to her desire to celebrate their twenty-fifth anniversary by going on a second honeymoon.

Archie. Wait a minute, Edith. Will you lay off that honeymoon stuff. Honeymoons is for kids not for older people like you.

Edith. Archie! Right now I am in the prime of my life and at the height of my sexual attractiveness.

Good for you, Edith. You're learning. By the way, Archie went on the second honeymoon, and they had a great time. They went to the same hotel in Atlantic City where they had spent their first honeymoon. They shared some beautiful memories and then received a surprise bottle of champagne from Mike and Gloria while Edith was getting ready for bed. I hope you recall the scene because it was beautiful.

(Archie pours champagne into glass. Edith enters from bathroom. She is wearing a beautiful nightgown and her lovely new negligee. She is radiant. Archie's back is to her.)

Edith. Here I am.

Archie. Gee, Edith, you look real nice. And you're wearin' the same thing you wore the first time I seen you comin' through that door.

Edith. No, Archie. I just bought this at Bloomingdales.

Archie. Ain't that funny! You look just like you did twenty-five years ago.

Edith. Oh, thank you, Archie.

Archie. Come on, let's kill this bottle of champagne.

Edith. Do you think that will be good for your stomach?

Archie. Why not? It's just like bicarb. It's got bubbles.

Edith. I'm gonna make a toast. Thank you for a wonderful twenty-five years.

Archie. You're welcome, Edith. And here's to you. I couldn't 'a done it without you.

   (They clink glasses and drink. They set the glasses down and look at each other awkwardly.)

Archie. Well, Edith?

Edith. Well what?

Archie. What do you say we go to bed now.

Edith. Oh, Archie. (They kiss, then embrace.)

Vernard Eller is right:

Sex is frosting; marriage (true marriage) is cake. Frosting is good; cake is good; but frosted cake is much better than either alone; they are made for each other.[1]

   Yes, sex not only makes the cake beautiful, it helps to hold it together. Thank God!

"Frosting on the cake."

8

To Be a
Loving Person

A little poem I hope never to forget is this short verse by Edwin
Markham:

> He drew a circle that shut me out.
> Heretic, rebel, a thing to flout.
> But love and I had the wit to win,
> We drew a circle that took him in.

Edith Bunker's whole life-style draws engulfing circles of love.
Whoever comes into her presence is touched by her enabling love
whether it is a burglar caught red-handed by her early return
home or her uptight, bigoted husband. In a day when "What the
World Needs Now Is Love, Sweet Love" is becoming an old song
that seems to have been sung by everybody but heard by nobody,
it behooves us to take a look at any human being who knows how
to love.

One distinctive of Edith Bunker's brand of love is the ability to
see behind the facades other human beings build for themselves.
Because she can see behind Archie's facade, she understands
Archie and can pass on this understanding to others, for example, to Mike:

Edith. Mike . . ., out there I told you why you yell at Archie. Don't you
wanna hear why Archie yells at you?

Mike. Ma, I know why he yells at me. He hates me.

Edith. Oh, no. Mike he yells at you because he's jealous of you.

Mike. I don't want to listen to this.

Edith. No. Wait a minute. You listen to me. He is jealous of you. And that
ain't hard to understand. Mike, you're going to college and you got your
whole future ahead of you. Archie had to quit school to support his
family, and he ain't never going to be nothin' more than he is right now.
But you've got a chance to be anything you want to be. That's why
Archie's jealous of you. He sees in you all the things he could never be.
So the next time Archie yells at you, try to be a little more understanding.

Edith's loving eyes can always look deep enough into another
individual to find a person. When she meets an old friend at a
high-school class reunion, it is almost as if she doesn't see that
he has become unattractively obese:

Edith. Buck, I'd know you anywhere . . . I can still see way inside you. See
Archie, ain't he a beautiful person?

Archie. Edith, I'll never figure you out. You and me can look at the same
guy, and you see a beautiful person and I see a blimp.

Edith: Yeah, ain't it too bad!

Archie has hit it on the head. He has described the basic difference between the two of them, and Edith is right—it is too bad!
It's too bad for Archie who in his blindness doesn't get to enjoy
the beauty of another person. And it's too bad for others around
him who must live with their beauty unrecognized and be
treated as less than persons.

Archie judges. Edith understands. And the rest of the people in
the world seem to line up behind one or the other. The question
is, Which line is longer? My fear is that Archie's is.

Another distinctive feature of Edith's love is that it is both
verbal and active. Words of love ooze across some people's lips
only to be invalidated by their actions. Other people live in a
loving way but never allow the words "I love you" to cross their

lips. If I had to choose, I would take the latter, but complete love includes both saying and doing.

On the day that Louise, Edith's long-time next-door neighbor, moved away, Edith went over five different times to tell her good-bye. The fifth time she took a gift of fruit with these parting words, "Louise, did I ever tell you I love you?" To which Louise responded, "Every minute we spent together." Acting it out had been important, but saying it and letting her friend hear it was also important.

Father John Powell tells about a beautiful friendship between two brother priests which ended in tragedy when one was hit by a car and killed. When told, the other ran to the scene, broke through the crowd of onlookers and police, and kneeling at the side of his friend took the lifeless body in his arms and cried out, "Don't die! You can't die! I never told you that I loved you."[1]

Many of us would have to respond in the same way should the same thing happen to us, but not Edith. She told Louise that she loved her.

Edith's love also often serves those from whom she can expect nothing in return. This kind of love is the costliest, and Edith expresses it in her service at the home for the aged. In a society that has to bribe people to be generous with charity balls, tax deductions, and raffles, it is refreshing to see a person who serves for one simple reason: "I care. Some of them old people are so lonely, they ain't got nobody."

Even though Edith expects nothing in return, this kind of love has its serendipities. Her cup of joy was overflowing at the end of one day at the home:

Edith. You know what happened today? Mr. Belfield tied his shoelaces.
Archie. Terrific. Who's Mr. Belfield?
Edith. Mr. Belfield is eighty-eight years old . . .
Archie. Oh, that's who he is!
Edith. . . . and he ain't tied his shoelaces in seven years. But today he did it for me.

"Louise, did I ever tell you I love you?"

Unexpected joy for one who cared, expecting nothing in return. But that is not where the story ends. It concludes with an even greater expression of joy:

Edith. Guess what, Archie? I ain't a volunteer no more . . . 'cause the home don't want me to be a volunteer no more. They like my work so much, startin' tomorrow they're gonna pay me two dollars an hour.

This final reaction, delight over money she is going to receive, creates a problem, especially in the context of discussing service that expects nothing in return. Women do a fantastic amount of volunteer work; they make our world a better place to live. The Bureau of Labor Statistics has said that "this country couldn't run without the unpaid, unsung, almost entirely female volunteer force."[2] I would like to see more women and many more men added to that volunteer force. Volunteers presently deal with the problems which the nurturing side of human personality handles. That side is active in most women and needs to be developed in most men.

But can our present value system contribute to the growth of volunteerism? Our society seems to be deciding values by dollar amounts. This is Archie's philosophy, and he represents a great number of people.

Edith. I gotta be doing something useful.
Archie. Like what? Givin' old geezers shoelace lessons and pushin' old bags into the shower! Bein' useful is bein' home. Tell me this, Florence Nighting-gown, how much are they payin' you for your sunshine?
Edith. Nothing.
Archie. Nothin'! Which is exactly what you're worth 'cause if you was doin' somethin', they'd be payin' you somethin'.

The philosophy, "If you was doing something, they would be paying you something," and its extension, "The more you get paid the more significant your job is and the more you are

"They're gonna pay me."

worth," symbolize the kind of attitude that can lead to destruction.

Must we put a dollar sign on everything? Many men answered this question a long time ago with a great big yes and have bet their fulfillment by going after the biggest possible sum of dollars. Some women have bought into that system. Could that be the case with Edith? Has she sold out to a system that puts a dollar sign on everything? The question is a worthwhile one but the answer is clear. Edith has not sold out; she was doing volunteer work long before she getting paid and she will continue to help people for the right reasons. She knows and is commited to the fulfillment gained when one human life touches another with a helping hand. You can't buy that kind of fulfillment with dollars.

Yet it is important to point out why Edith was so elated when the Home was going to pay her. "They like my work so much, startin' tomorrow they're gonna pay me two dollars an hour." For Edith I don't believe it was the two dollars as much as it was an affirmation that she was doing a significant thing. She saw the money as society's way of showing appreciation for her and her work.

This is not to suggest that the monetary value of the dollars received by Edith is insignificant. Those dollars can create for Edith a new kind of independence that is necessary for her wholeness.

Many married women suffer because they never have a dollar that they can, in their own minds, truly call their own. Some men have forgotten what it is like to be in that position and we need to be reminded again of how important it is for an individual to have money that is his or her own and for which they do not have to be accountable to anyone. My wife tells me she feels silly buying me a gift with money that I have earned whereas she finds it very meaningful to buy the gift with money she has earned. I can understand that and I am concerned that women not only have opportunities to earn but that when they do that they receive a fair compensation for the job done, one equivalent to what a man would receive for doing the same job.

However, women can help men find some values without dollar signs. They need to come into our competitive world and teach us how to cooperate. We have had enough hard-driving, dog-eat-dog "road to success," and we just might be ready for nurturing, caring, cooperating style if someone would show us the way. If someone like Edith would show us how to draw those engulfing circles of love in either volunteer or paid work.

9

Fighting Fair

Being a caring, loving, servant-type person does not mean being a doormat. Yes, we have a great responsibility for others, but we also have a responsibility to ourselves. A balanced life necessitates tension between self and others, to lose that tension is to lose wholeness. Leaning too far to the "other" side can create a kind of spiritual masochism; leaning too far to the "self" side is a good way, according to the late Halford E. Luccock, "to make a mummy of yourself."

The best preserved thing in all history is an Egyptian mummy. The surest way to make a mummy of yourself is to give all your attention to preserving your life.[1]

Edith is in no danger of making a mummy of herself, but she may court the tendency to become a doormat. She is to be affirmed for taking such good care of others, but she needs to be encouraged to take good care of herself. It would be good for Edith and others in her situation to hear these words of Charlotte Clinebell:

Whether or not I *was* responsible for [my family's] unhappiness, I *felt* responsible. The ideal woman keeps her family happy and successful. What an impossible burden to bear! . . . What I realize now as I look back is that I wasn't such a bad wife or such a bad mother—though I made a lot of mistakes—or even such an inadequate woman. What I didn't do such a good job of was being me.[2]

After hearing a speech at a woman's meeting, Edith said it another way:

Edith. Archie, am I being fulfilled? Is my role in life to be determined by an accident of birth? To the world, I'm a woman; to you, I'm a housewife; to Gloria, I'm a mother, but who am I to me?

She must answer that question, and she can only do so by becoming responsible for herself. Nobody else can do it for her. A lot of us are in situations where the only answer for our predicament is to become responsible for ourselves. This is the significance of the Biblical story of the man by the pool of Bethesda who had been ill for thirty-eight years (see John 5:1–9). Can you believe it! Jesus asked him if he wanted to be healed! He seems to have known that a lot of us get more mileage from being sick than from being healthy. Sickness can be a great way to escape responsibility, which must be why Jesus paid no attention to the man's excuse that he had nobody to put him in the pool. Instead, Jesus told him, "Rise, take up your bed and walk." A fair paraphrase would be, "Get up and get going." The man did just that, and he was healed.

Jesus was saying what a lot of us need to hear. We expect the fairy godmother to solve our problems, but she is not coming. Healing will occur only when we become responsible for ourselves. It took the man by the pool thirty-eight years to step out on his own. Certainly he was impowered by Jesus, the Significant Other, but ultimately it was up to him.

Many women have been victimized for many years by a stifling society, but now there are some significant others who will stand by them if they will become responsible for themselves. The question is, How do you do that? One way is to become responsible for yourself by learning how to be assertive. The word *assertive* has recently become identified most closely with a psychological method called Systematic Assertive Therapy. Many women have been helped to move from doormat to whole person with the help of assertiveness training, a phrase to which I at first reacted negatively.

Assertiveness sounded harsh until I read *The New Assertive Woman* by Lynn Z. Bloom, Karen Coburn, and Joan Pearlman. I learned that assertiveness is the "golden mean" between *aggressiveness,* which victimized, and *nonassertiveness,* which is victimized. That makes me think of Edith and how many times she has been victimized by Archie the aggressive. She could benefit from what the authors call "Everywoman's Bill of Rights." All of us, men and women, can be helped to wholeness by considering these personal rights.

Everywoman's Bill of Rights

1. The right to be treated with respect.
2. The right to have and express your own feelings and opinions.
3. The right to be listened to and taken seriously.
4. The right to set your own priorities.
5. The right to say no without feeling guilty.
6. The right to ask for what you want.
7. The right to get what you pay for.
8. The right to ask for information from professionals.
9. The right to make mistakes.
10. The right to choose not to assert yourself.[3]

Edith Bunker is beginning to claim some of these rights for herself. During the past year, people who had read *God, Man, and Archie Bunker* have often told me they thought Archie and Edith had been changing over the years. I agree. Archie is becoming more tender, and Edith is becoming more assertive—an improvement in both cases.

At times, Edith has actually been aggressive. Probably the world will never forget the night she slapped Archie for gambling. Later on she apologized for hitting him but explained that gambling had been such a problem in the past that it had almost

"The right to—"

destroyed them and their marriage. She had never talked about it before and only shared one incident with Gloria:

Edith. I'll never forget when we was living on Union Street and we had this used car. Well, one day I was looking out the window, and I saw this man driving off in our car. I yelled to Archie, "Archie, there's a man stealing our car!" And he said, "Let him have it, Edith. I lost it to him last night."

All the pain of past came back when she found he had started gambling again; so she slapped him, then apologized, and then, rather than pulling into a shell of shame, she stood up to Archie in a health-producing assertive way:

Archie. You hit me, and you hurt me. Did I ever hit you, for any reason?

Edith. I never gave you any reason.

Archie. That don't make no difference!

Edith. Archie, I could forgive you for hitting me, but I don't think I can ever forgive you for making me hit you. . . . Archie, can I read you something?

Archie. No, I want an apology.

Edith. This is an apology.

Archie. Well, all right. I didn't tell you you had to write it all out, but if it's an apology. Go ahead. Read it.

Edith. (Takes a letter out of apron pocket and reads) I'm sorry for what I have done. I don't know how I could have did such a terrible thing to someone who's been so good to me. I promise never to do it again. I hope you can forgive me.

Archie. Good. That ain't the fanciest writin' in the world, but then you ain't no Henry Woolworth Longfellow, but it's an apology and I accept it.

Edith. I didn't write this, Archie, you did.

Archie. I what?

Edith. Yeah. Twenty years ago, when I was gonna leave you, because you was gambling. You wrote this . . . So, all you have to do is change the date on this letter, and sign it . . . And while you're signing it, I'll tell you how sorry I am that I hit you.

Much to Edith's delight, he signed it. So she benefitted by being assertive, but Archie benefitted most, she provided strength for his weakness.

There are other examples of Edith's increasing assertiveness, such as the night Archie said he didn't want to take her out. She accepted the fact that he wouldn't and went by herself—to Kelsey's Tavern where she made quite a hit. But more than that she made quite an impression on Archie, and now he takes her out more often.

The Bunkers' second honeymoon happened because an assertive woman wanted to "keep her marriage fresh."

Edith. I was in the dentist's office, reading this article in *Cosmopolitan* magazine, "Ten Modern Ways to Keep Your Marriage Fresh." Well, the first nine ways was a little too fresh for Archie. But the last one said— "Go on a second honeymoon and feel like a newlywed again." And that's what we're gonna do.

They did it, and again Archie was glad.

What is causing this change in Edith? Where is she learning assertiveness? Partly it's a matter of Edith's self-survival, and partly it's due to her sensitivity to the new trends of our times. But Mike and Gloria have been significant models in supporting and encouraging Edith. Even when their methods sound extreme, she is impressed enough with their continuing relationship to glean what she might apply to her marriage. And she listens when they offer advice.

Gloria. . . . when something bothers you, you shouldn't keep it bottled up. You've got to get it out. That's what Michael and I have been doing recently . . . We're trying something psychologists call fair fighting. They're telling people to let off steam, get things out in the open. When you keep things bottled up inside, it's called gunny-sacking and that's not healthy. Some couples are even taking lessons in fighting.

Edith. Oh, Archie don't need no lessons.

Edith is right, "Archie don't need no lessons," but neither does she need to keep things bottled up, including the beautiful person she is. She listened to Gloria and took charge that night. In doing so she grew, Archie grew, and their marriage grew. Edith

"You don't have to lie down and let bad things walk over you."

is growing, but often she, like many women, has been the victim. These words of Art Greer should reassure them:

You don't have to lie down and let bad things walk over you. You are as potent as they are: more potent, often. Take charge! Take the good things you understand and use them to wipe out the things that make life insufferable for you.[4]

10

The Late Bloomer

Edith has a party and introduces her new friend who tells the guests, with all the fervor of a Billy Graham:

There are three things a woman remembers all her life. Her wedding night, the birth of her first child, and her first Tupperware party.

Makes you wonder what else there is to live for if you have, as Edith already had, all three of these experiences. Sounds silly; yet some women come to a point in their lives, sometime after marriage, when they decide it is going to be downhill the rest of the way, that life is behind and death is ahead. They stop growing and start shrinking. Shrinking is the byproduct of living in a rut, and with Gloria and Mike gone and always in danger of moving even farther away, Edith partially describes the rut as "dinner at six, Cronkite at seven, and bed at 10:30."

She expresses to Archie the cry of many women:

Edith. . . . you go to work and that leaves me alone with nothing to do all day and nothing to look forward to.

These are the words of a woman headed for trouble. Our land knows many such women. Some become alcoholics, others are appendages to a hard-driving career men, and still others just shrink and die long before they enter the grave.

There is, however, an option: growth. Growth is really what life is all about, for when we cease to grow, we cease to live.

Edith is at that point in life where she finally has time for the growth which Mildred Newman and Bernard Berkowitz describe as "doing things you've never done before, sometimes things you once didn't even dream you could do."[1] This is a good definition, but "doing things you once didn't even dream you could do" doesn't mean there was no dreaming because growth is preceded by dreaming. People who don't dream don't grow. (I am talking now about dreaming in the sense of hopeful planning mixed with a bit of fantasy rather than what you do when you are asleep.)

The problem is that the stifling process of which Edith has been a victim for so many years kills dreams and dulls the imagination. The Man of La Mancha is right: "To surrender dreams, this may be madness."[2] Edith must be encouraged to dream again, to think of those things she would like to do, try, accomplish, perfect, and experience. Growth is the process of of blooming, and the goal of life is to flower completely.

How can a person like Edith keep on budding and sprouting new growth? First, you must have the desire, and then you need to know your gifts. More generally that means to be sure to recognize everything you have going for you. Dr. Theodore Isaac Rubin calls this process "recognizing your assets"—health, home, parents, family, emotional freedom, privacy, possessions, attractiveness, uniqueness, brains, imagination, creativity, experience, feelings, toleration, empathy, skills, and so on.[3]

Many of the above can be seen as either assets or liabilities. How you see them is often a matter of attitude. This is where Edith has an advantage because she operates from a base of gratitude; often what others might see as a liability, she sees as an asset. For example, when Gloria, staggering from the blows of inflation, exclaims, "I don't know how you manage to make ends meet, Ma," Edith says, "I'm lucky, I was brought up in the depression."

I hope she can have that same attitude about her age in spite of our culture's emphasis on youthfulness. When it comes to living the full life, age is an asset. A few years ago *Time* magazine spoke of the fascination of a middle-aged woman being

the distillation of glamour into poise, inner amusement and enriched femininity no twenty-year-old sex kitten has lived long enough to acquire . . . The young laugh at the way things seem; middle age laughs at the way things are. The young want to dynamite the treasure vaults of life; middle age has learned the combination. The young think they know; the middle age knows that no one knows.[4]

Age is a great asset. More of us past forty need to act our age with pride and vigor.

The biblical concept of gifts is another way of referring to assets. We are gifted by God. God gives each of us unique and special gifts. Our responsibility is to use them and not waste them. Furthermore, the biblical view of interdependence is that we have a responsibility to encourage one another to use our respective gifts. It's too bad that we have often not only not encouraged women to use all their gifts but have discouraged and prohibited them.

Another aid to growth is the support of some significant other or others who will enable, encourage, listen, reinforce, care, and call you forth. Ideally, Archie could be one of these people to Edith. Since that doesn't seem likely at this point, she must, rather than going it alone, find a group with whom she can meet regularly. In these group meetings she and the other members could ascertain their assets, set their goals, and report their progress or their defeats—in a climate of acceptance.

Edith says she is alone, but she needs to know she is not alone in her loneliness. Many like her would respond if someone were to say, "C'mon, let's grow together."

Growing has to do with doing. If you want to grow, you have to do something about it. It doesn't just happen. First, think about what you are going to do, then take pencil and paper (a journal would be better so you could do it regularly) and write down the areas in which you would like to grow, the kind of growth you would like to see, and how you are going to make it happen. Listen closely to yourself, and, rather than being embarrassed, respond to your deepest desires. If Edith listened closely to herself she would hear, "So wouldn't you like to take up playing the piano again? When you were a child, you learned to play the 'Minute Waltz' in 7½ minutes. Wouldn't you like to improve on that?" If she hears such a voice, why not respond?

And she should respond to any other voices she hears whether they speak of travel, education, career, or creativity. She has a lot of gifts, and there are a myriad of possibilities, but she must decide.

There are two kinds of people in our world: those who think about doing and those who do. A lot of doers never had a choice in the first place. For example, most of us men knew we were going to have to be breadwinners, and so going to work, in a lot of cases, was a matter of survival. We never had the choice of "to work or not to work."

It is not so with many women. Because they have the choice, they are never pressed to make the choice. That's why it is necessary to decide what you want to do, share that decision with some significant others, and then ask their support in helping you fulfill your desire.

Remember, we are in the middle of a revolution that is slowly bringing about equal rights and equal opportunity for women. It is not yet completed, but the opportunities are greater now than they were. Women have never had so many options for growth, and when one woman acts on her option, the revolution benefits because that one encourages the many.

So bloom, Edith, and remember it is never too late. They called Eleanor Roosevelt a late bloomer, and we could use a few more Eleanor Roosevelts.

11

Edith the Good

There was a day when Archie's major criticism of Edith was that she was too good. When he crowned her "Edith the Good," his intent was to degrade her. But as he has continued to live with this woman, he has not only come to respect her goodness but to expect it. That is why it was hard for him to believe his ears:

Edith. I was arrested.
Archie. You was what?
Edith. I was arrested.
Archie. Arrested . . . What happened?
Edith. It'll just make you mad, Archie.
Archie. It won't make me mad! Tell me!!
Edith. Well, I don't know where to begin.
Archie. At the beginning.
Edith. Well, this morning, after I went upstairs and sorted the laundry, I came down to do the breakfast dishes, and . . .
Archie. Hold it . . . forget the beginnin'. Start at the end.
Edith. I was arrested.
Archie. Edith, can't you just tell me how the trouble started?
Edith. The trouble started with our old apartment on Union Square—it was on Number 44 bus route. Remember Archie? The apartment where it got so hot in the summer, Arthur always had to sleep on the escape? (to Mike) Arthur was our cat. Archie didn't like Arthur very much, did you, Archie?
Archie. I hated his guts. Get on with it.
Edith. Well, the trouble was, the Number 44 bus don't go to Bayside and I told the little old lady it did!!

Archie. Who???

Edith. The one in Wellington's Department Store who wanted to go to Bayside. I told her Number 44.

Archie. So you told the lady wrong. They can't arrest you for that. What was the charge?

Edith. The charge was, I was wearing the wig!!

Archie. The wig?! . . . What wig?

Edith. The one I was trying on at Wellington's. And I was still wearing it when I ran out of the store after the old lady, to tell her it was the wrong bus.

Archie. Edith, if you ran out of the store with a wig on, they'd arrest you for shopliftin'.

Edith. That was the charge.

She then breaks into tears, and Archie goes into his usual self-centered tirade, complaining how his credit is going to be ruined. Edith responds with a sobbing, "I'm sorry, Archie."

Then he speaks with respect and with a degree of insight not previously exhibited.

Archie. All right, all right, Edith. It ain't your fault. It's the rest of the world.

Edith. What do you mean?

Archie. I mean the world ain't ready for ya', Edith, that's all . . . What I am trying to say, Edith, is that I know you ain't never hurt nobody and you ain't never lied to nobody and I'm damn sure you never stole nothin' from nobody, neither.

I never thought I would hear Archie say it: "The world ain't ready for you, Edith, that's all."

Is Archie right? Is the world ready for Edith Bunker, "Edith the Good"? Does he mean that our kind of world doesn't know how to handle a person as good as Edith? That Edith is too unbelievable for the so-called permissive society? That she is too easily bruised by the daily bumps and scrapes of amoral people? If this is what he means, I agree. But in a different sense our world is ready and ripe for an Edith Bunker because we just plain need some good people. We need people who will care so much about a little old lady catching a bus that they forget their consumer habit and rush to help. We need people who won't lie, won't cheat, and won't steal. We need all the "Ediths the Good" we can get. To such people we need to say loud and clear that it is OK to be good. But isn't that understood? Does it have to be said? Yes, it needs to be said because there are rumblings that being good is not OK. In some circles it is almost embarrassing to be known as a good person. It's more acceptable to be immoral. Concern for survival behooves us to ask, What is so bad about being good? and, What is so good about being bad? A positive answer to the first should eliminate any need to ask the second.

How could Archie think he was insulting Edith by calling her "Edith the Good"? Maybe it is because he misunderstands "goodness." Undoubtedly he has been the victim of either some self-righteous prude (the kind of person Mark Twain referred to as "being good in the worst sense of the world") or he has been conned into thinking that being too good would somehow deny his masculinity. It is probably both, compounded by the thinking of a society that berates people by calling them do-gooders.

It is time we resurrected the word and the concept of *good* by rediscovering its biblical meaning. In the Old Testament the Hebrew word for good is *tov,* and it means pleasant, joyful, and enjoyable. That fits Edith.

In the New Testament the word *good* is a translation of one of two Greek words: *kalos* or *agathos.* Both are popular New Testament words with *kalos* being used over one hundred times. Dr. Barclay says it is hard to find the exact English equivalent. *Winsomeness* comes close, but the best translation is the Scot's word *bonnie.* Dr. Barclay describes *bonnie* with a story about the Scottish preacher, J. P. Struthers. Struthers lived at the end of a road by the hillside frequented each evening by courting young people. In the late afternoon before the evening passers-by came, Struthers would pick flowers from his garden and make little bouquets which he would place on the garden wall so the young men could give them to the young ladies they were courting. That was, Dr. Barclay says, a *bonnie* thing to do.[1]

There is a moral concern about Edith that is not prudish but winsome, in a word, bonnie. That is good.

The other Greek word *agathos* refers more to the ethical spirit. In this sense, Dr. Albert Schweitzer was called a "good" man. On his only visit to America he received the celebrity treatment and was usually surrounded by newspeople as he was one day on a Chicago railroad station platform. Beyond the press he noticed a poor old woman laden with suitcases. His automatic response was to excuse himself from the group, take the woman's bags, and help her onto the train and safely to her seat. He then rejoined the newspeople.[2]

That is good. What is so bad about being good?

Our nation was founded by, among others, the Puritans, a good people. But they have been misunderstood, partially because Hugh Hefner confused them with the Victorians when writing his Playboy philosophy. The Puritans were not killjoys but persons with a moral stamina that seems obsolete in our day. They had a "tender conscience and a kind of moral sensitivity and integrity, a fine-grained sense of honor and trustworthiness which gave body to American community life."[3] That's good.

Good people make the world a better place to live, but where will they come from? "Kickbacks, payoffs, consumer fraud, illegal competition, insurance fraud, embezzlement, and other white collar crimes cost the American public over 40 billion dollars a year."[4] Where are these people who are going to make the world a better place to live? We keep waiting for a leader, but we forget Will Rogers' warning: "If we ever pass on as a great nation, we ought to put on our tombstone 'America died from a delusion that she had moral leadership.' "[5]

We can't wait any longer. We will have to turn to the little people, the little good people.

Americans have a rather simple but effective way of evaluating people. They ask, "Would you buy a used car from this person?" When I hear that question, I think of Edith and the time Archie told her he didn't want her cousin Estelle and Ralph visiting from Philadelphia after she had already invited them:

Gloria: Ma, if you've already invited them, what are you going to do?

Edith: Well, I wrote 'em a letter saying the house was being painted, the plumbing didn't work and the furnace was broken down. . . . 'cause Archie told me to. . . . But when I read it over, I tore it up, 'cause I could see right through me.

I'd buy a used car from Edith the Good. There is one problem though. I understand that as women gain equality with men the crime rate among women is increasing. I had hoped it would be the other way around.

12

What Are You Doing the Rest of Your Life?

Well, Edith, there are your ten giant steps. Actually they aren't all giant steps, are they? Some of the "permissions" are really affirmations, beautiful parts of you that need to be recognized and developed even further. I hope mentioning them will encourage you.

I especially hope that nothing I have said has negated the beautiful person you are and the even more beautiful person you are becoming. I have encouraged you to step out in new directions, but you have shown great strength in many areas I've not mentioned.

The way you stuck with Archie during his gambling problems reminded us all of the responsibility of the strong to the weak. The way you were so honest about both your strength and weakness when you discovered the lump in your breast enabled women all over America to face that same experience with a new sense of hope and understanding.

And what a beautiful mother you have been to Gloria! She is evidence of your freeing kind of love. How fortunate little Joey is to be the recipient of that same kind of love from his grandmother.

Remember the old word association game where you are supposed to respond with the first word that comes to mind when a certain word is said? For example, if you said *black* to me, I would probably respond with *white*. Well, the word that comes to mind whenever I hear your name is *hospitality,* not the dictionary definition of *hospitality* but Henri Nouwen's:

Hospitality, therefore, means primarily the creation of a free space where the stranger can enter and become a friend instead of an enemy. Hospitality is not to change people, but to offer them space where change can take place. It is not to bring men and women over to our side but to offer freedom not disturbed by dividing lines. It is not to lead our neighbor into a corner where there are no alternatives left but to open a wide spectrum of options for choice and commitment. Hospitality is not a subtle invitation to adopt the life style of the host, but the gift of the chance for the guest to find his own.[1]

I guess that's why it feels so good to be around you.

It is amazing all that you are in spite of your stifling environment. How exciting it is to think of the fulfillment of your potential as you take giant steps toward destiflization. I hope you won't linger; I hope the rest of your life won't be wasted.

Some steps are risky, but whenever you feel hesitant, remember that no matter how many "stifles" you hear alot of folks are on your side. More important, God is on your side, and he has been liberating people a long time.

There will be struggles and barriers and setbacks, but don't let them stop you or keep you from enjoying the journey. It is not always necessary to keep the roadrunner pace. That is why I leave you with the words of Brother Jeremiah:

If I had my life to live over again, I'd try to make more mistakes next time. I would relax. I would limber up. I would be sillier than I have been this trip. I know of very few things I would take seriously. I would take more trips. I would climb more mountains, swim more rivers, and watch more sunsets. I would do more walking and looking. I would eat more ice cream and less beans. I would have more actual troubles and fewer imaginary ones.

You see, I am one of those people who live prophylactically and sensibly and sanely, hour and hour, day after day. Oh, I've had my moments and if I had it to do over again, I'd have more of them. In fact, I'd try to have nothing else. Just moments, one after another, instead of living so many years ahead each day. I have been one of those people who never go anywhere without a thermometer, a hot water bottle, a gargle, a raincoat, aspirin, and a parachute. If I had it to do over again, I would go places, do things and travel lighter than I have.

If I had my life to live over, I would start barefooted earlier in the spring and stay that way later in the fall. I would play hooky more. I would ride on more merry-go-rounds. I'd pick more daisies.[2]

God bless you, Edith.

Notes

CHAPTER 1

1. Pauline Bart, *Trans-action*, vol. 8, Nov.-Dec. 1970.

CHAPTER 2

1. John Powell, *The Secret of Staying in Love* (Niles, IL: Argus, 1974), p. 13.
2. Erich Fromm, Excerpts from *The Art of Loving,* vol. 9 in World Perspectives. Edited by Ruth Nanda Anshen. Copyrighted 1956 by Erich Fromm. By permission of Harper & Row; also reprinted with permission by George Allen and Unwin, Ltd., London.

CHAPTER 3

1. Alan Grabner, *After Eve* (Minneapolis: Augsburg, 1972), p. 18
2. Charlotte Holt Clinebell, *Meet Me in the Middle* (New York: Harper & Row, 1973), p. 14.
3. Irene Claremont de Castillejo, *Knowing Woman* (New York: Harper & Row, 1973), p. 15.
4. John Powell, *The Secret of Staying in Love* (Niles, IL: Argus, 1974), p. 62.

CHAPTER 4

1. Marabel Morgan, *The Total Woman* (Fleming Revell, 1973; Pocket Books, 1975), p. 13
2. Ibid., Part II, pp. 51–107.

3. Carl Rogers, *Becoming Partners* (New York: Dell, 1972), p. 209.

4. Harry Stack Sullivan, *Conceptions of Modern Psychology* (New York: W.W. Norton & Co., 1953), pp. 42–43.

5. Charlotte Holt Clinebell, *Meet Me In the Middle* (New York: Harper & Row, 1973), Prologue XIII.

6. Kahlil Gibran, *The Prophet* (New York, Alfred A. Knopf, 1923), p. 15.

CHAPTER 5

1. Kathryn Lindskoog, *Up From Eden* (Elgin, IL: David C. Cook Publishing Co., 1976), pp. 89–91.

2. Alan Graebner, *After Eve* (Minneapolis: Augsburg, 1972), p. 26.

3. R. Lofton Hudson, *Grace Is Not a Blue-Eyed Blond* (Waco, Texas: Word Books, 1968), p. 32.

CHAPTER 6

1. H. L. Mencken, *Woman's Role in Contemporary Society* (New York: Avon Books, 1972).

CHAPTER 7

1. Vernard Eller, *The Mad Morality* (Nashville & New York: Abingdon, 1970).

CHAPTER 8

1. John Powell, *The Secret of Staying In Love* (Niles, IL: Argus, 1974), p. 122.

2. Quoted in "What Every Intelligent Man Should Know About Women," by Pat Collins, an article in *Mainliner Magazine,* June, 1976.

3. Edwin Markham, "Outwitted" *The Shoes of Happiness* (New York: Doubleday, Doran, 1928) p. 1.

CHAPTER 9

1. Halford E. Luccock, *Context,* Claretian Publications, Chicago, 1 March 1976.
2. Charlotte Clinebell, *Meet Me In the Middle* (New York: Harper & Row, 1973).
3. Lynn Z. Bloom, Karen Coburn, Joan Pearlman, *The New Assertive Woman* (New York: Delacorte Press, 1975).
4. Art Greer, *No Grown-Ups in Heaven* (New York: Hawthorn Books, 1975).

CHAPTER 10

1. Mildred Newman and Bernard Berkowitz, *How To Be Your Own Best Friend* (New York: Random House, 1971).
2. *Man of La Mancha* by Dale Wasserman, Mitch Leigh; Lyrics by Joe Darion, Published by Random House, New York.
3. Theodore Isaac Rubin, *The Winner's Notebook* (New York: Macmillan, 1967), pp. 1–37.
4. *Time*, 29 July 1966.

CHAPTER 11

1. William Barclay, *New Testament Words* (Philadelphia: Westminister Press, 1964).
2. Waldo Beach, *The Christian Life, Teacher's Book* (Richmond, VA: CLC Press, 1966).
3. Ibid.
4. *White Collar Crime*, U.S. Chamber of Commerce.